CTRL+ALT=WEALTH

UNLOCKING THE POWER OF ALTERNATIVE INVESTMENTS

SIDDA RAVITEJA

Made with ❤ on the Notion Press Platform
www.notionpress.com

Contents

Foreword — vii

Preface — ix

Acknowledgements — xi

1. Ctrl: Taking Control Of Your Wealth — 1

2. Alt: The Alternative Advantage — 6

3. Why Alternatives Are Undervalued — 12

4. Private Equity And Venture Capital — 18

5. Real Estate Beyond Housing — 24

6. Commodities And Precious Metals — 30

7. Collectibles And Passion Investments — 35

8. Risk Vs. Reward In Alternatives — 40

9. Starting Small: Entry Points For Beginners — 45

10. Blending Traditional And Alternative Investments — 50

11. Economic Trends Shaping Alternatives — 54

12. Ctrl+Alt: Planning For Long-Term Wealth — 59

13. Invoice Discounting: Unlocking Immediate — 64

14. Peer-to-Peer Lending Platforms: Democratizing — 67

15. The Golden Rule – Understanding Risks Before You Invest — 70

Foreword

Traditional investment avenues are no longer the only path to wealth creation in today's fast-evolving financial landscape. As global markets shift, economic uncertainties rise, and technology disrupts industries, investors—especially those from middle-class backgrounds—seek more innovative, diverse ways to grow their wealth. Alternative investments are no longer exclusive to the ultra-rich; they are now accessible, practical, and, in many cases, highly rewarding.

Ctrl+Alt=Wealth guides the modern Indian investor beyond conventional stocks and real estate. This book illuminates various alternative investments—from private equity and invoice discounting to cryptocurrencies and collectibles—breaking them down into simple, actionable insights.

Raviteja brings a wealth of knowledge and a deep understanding of overlooked financial opportunities. With its clear, structured approach, this book challenges common myths, highlights emerging trends, and provides practical strategies for anyone looking to diversify their investment portfolio.

Whether you are just starting your financial journey or looking to expand your portfolio beyond traditional assets, Ctrl+Alt=Wealth will help you navigate the exciting world of alternative investments with confidence and clarity.

— Dr.Gurunath Sidda
Founder of Visishta Nature Cure and
Author of Life in Balance (A Blueprint for Ultimate
Human Health)

Preface

The idea for Ctrl+Alt=Wealth was born out of a simple realization—most middle-class investors in India still rely on traditional investment options like fixed deposits, gold, and real estate, often missing out on high-growth opportunities in alternative investments. While alternative assets such as private equity, invoice discounting, peer-to-peer lending, and cryptocurrencies have been gaining traction globally, they remain largely unexplored by many everyday investors.

Having spent years studying market trends and financial strategies, I wanted to create a guide that simplifies these concepts and makes them accessible to the common investor. This book is not about overnight riches or speculative trading; rather, it is about understanding new investment avenues, diversifying intelligently, and building sustainable wealth over time.

I have tailored this book specifically for Indian investors, focusing on practical, real-world insights that can help middle-class families, professionals, and young investors make informed financial decisions. Each chapter breaks down a different asset class, highlighting its risks, rewards, and the best ways to get started.

This book is not just a financial guide—it is a mindset shift. The world of investing is evolving, and those who adapt early will have the greatest advantage. If you've ever felt limited by traditional investment choices or wanted to explore new opportunities but didn't know where to start, this book is for you.

I hope Ctrl+Alt=Wealth helps you take control of your financial future, unlock alternative paths to prosperity, and ultimately achieve financial independence.

Happy investing!

-Sidda Raviteja

Acknowledgements

Writing Ctrl+Alt=Wealth has been an incredible journey, and it wouldn't have been possible without the support, guidance, and encouragement of many wonderful people.

First and foremost, I want to express my deepest gratitude to my lovely daughter, Aarna, whose curiosity, energy, and limitless potential inspire me every day. This book is dedicated to her and to the belief that the future belongs to those who seek knowledge and embrace opportunities.

A special thanks to my family for their unwavering love, patience, and encouragement throughout this process. Your belief in me has been my greatest strength.

To my friends, mentors, and colleagues, who have shared invaluable insights and experiences, thank you for pushing me to think bigger and go beyond conventional ideas. Your perspectives have helped shape the depth and clarity of this book.

I am also grateful to the financial experts, investors, and industry leaders whose work has provided inspiration and guidance. Their research, case studies, and real-world applications have played a key role in shaping the content of this book.

A heartfelt thank you to my readers—aspiring investors, professionals, and middle-class families—who are eager to explore new financial opportunities. This book is for you, and I hope it serves as a valuable resource in your journey toward financial growth and independence.

Finally, I want to acknowledge everyone who played a role—big or small—in making this book a reality. Your encouragement and belief in this project have been invaluable, and I am truly grateful.

With gratitude,
-Sidda Raviteja

CHAPTER ONE

CTRL: TAKING CONTROL OF YOUR WEALTH

1. Introduction: Why Control Matters

For many middle-class Indians, managing wealth often starts and ends with a bank account, Fixed Deposits (FDs), and possibly some insurance policies. The idea of taking control of wealth is foreign to a large part of the population. But as the world changes rapidly, relying solely on traditional savings is no longer enough to build lasting wealth. In fact, without actively managing your finances, you're likely missing out on growth opportunities.

Many people have an instinctive desire to ensure financial security, but security alone doesn't lead to wealth. Wealth creation is a conscious effort, a journey that requires knowledge, decision-making, and the courage to step beyond the conventional.

This chapter is about realizing that you can—and should—take control of your financial future. It's about making informed choices and expanding your horizons beyond just the familiar ways of saving and investing.

2. The Indian Middle-Class Mindset

The Indian middle class, a significant portion of the country's population, has traditionally gravitated toward investments that promise security above all else. For generations, Indians have trusted gold, Fixed Deposits, and Life Insurance Corporation (LIC) policies to secure their financial future. While these options offer safety, they are not necessarily the most effective at growing wealth over the long term.

Take gold, for example, a long-standing symbol of wealth in Indian culture. While gold often holds its value and can provide emotional satisfaction, its ability to outpace inflation and generate real wealth is limited. Similarly, FDs, once considered the safest investment, today yield returns that are lower than the rate of inflation, meaning your money is essentially losing value over time.

But there's a shift happening. As Indian middle-class families become more exposed to global investment opportunities and financial literacy rises, many are realizing that the security-first mentality is not enough to build lasting wealth. This chapter encourages you to break free from traditional thinking and take control of your financial destiny.

3. The Problem: Why Traditional Approaches Fall Short

Let's talk numbers for a second. The average Fixed Deposit in India offers an interest rate of around 5-6%. If we account for inflation, which hovers between 5-7%, your FD doesn't even keep pace with the cost of living. This is a perfect example of why the traditional approach isn't enough.

You may have put ₹1,00,000 in an FD for a year and earned ₹5,000-6,000 in interest, but the true value of your ₹1,00,000 has reduced due to inflation. In essence, you're saving but not growing. This may seem safe, but it is actually the opposite of wealth creation.

Another challenge is the over-reliance on salary income. While a stable job is a great foundation, it's a limited income source. It's important to realize that relying solely on your salary for financial growth is risky—especially with job market fluctuations and inflation pressures. This brings us to the key insight of this book: control your wealth by diversifying your sources of income.

4. Taking the First Step Toward Control

Mindset Shift: Thinking Beyond Security to Growth

The first step in taking control of your wealth is a mindset shift. You have to look beyond the comfort of a savings account or an FD and consider how to make your money work for you. The key is not just to save but to grow—make smart decisions with your savings that will generate returns over time.

To get started, think about opportunity cost. Simply put, every rupee you leave idle in your FD or savings account could have been invested elsewhere for better returns. A small mindset shift can lead to huge results over time.

Setting Clear Goals

Setting clear and achievable financial goals is crucial. For instance, setting a target to accumulate ₹30 lakh for your child's education in 10 years or growing your retirement fund to ₹50 lakh can help you stay focused. These goals will guide your investment decisions.

SMART Goals—Specific, Measurable, Achievable, Relevant, and Time-bound—are a practical tool here.

Instead of vague goals like "I want to save more money," aim for specific targets. For instance, "I want to invest ₹ 5,000 every month for the next 3 years into a balanced fund to build ₹2 lakh by 2027."

5. The Wealth Equation for Middle-Class Indians

One of the first steps toward taking control of your wealth is to adopt a simple equation:

Earnings – Savings = Spending

However, the key to financial control is reversing this equation:

Earnings – Spending = Savings

For many in the middle class, the reality is often the reverse: we spend first and save whatever is left over. By flipping the equation, we ensure that savings and investments become a priority. Try adopting the 50-30-20 rule:

50% of your income for essential needs (rent, food, utilities).

30% for discretionary spending (entertainment, travel, etc.).

20% toward investments and savings.

This small step will change your financial habits and put you in control.

6. Building a Financial Toolkit

Before diving into alternative investments, it's essential to have a solid financial foundation. This includes:

Emergency Fund: Always have a reserve of 6 months of expenses in a liquid, low-risk account like a savings account or liquid fund.

Insurance: Ensure you have the right health and life insurance to safeguard against unforeseen expenses. Opt for term insurance, which offers high coverage at low premiums.

Debt Management: Pay off high-interest loans first, as they reduce your ability to invest effectively.

These tools are your financial safety net, ensuring that you have control over your wealth and aren't making decisions in a panic when life throws curveballs.

7. Ending with Actionable Steps

Start by putting the following in place:

Review your expenses and investments every month.

Prioritize savings and set aside a fixed percentage of your income for investments.

Research at least one new investment option each week, starting with the basics of mutual funds, stocks, or ETFs.

Here's an actionable example: Start a Systematic Investment Plan (SIP) in an index fund or mutual fund that invests in real estate investment trusts (REITs), which will provide exposure to real estate with relatively low risk and small investment amounts.

CHAPTER TWO

ALT: THE ALTERNATIVE ADVANTAGE

1. Introduction: What Are Alternative Investments?

Alternative investments are any asset classes outside the traditional stock and bond market. These include real estate, private equity, hedge funds, cryptocurrencies, commodities, art, and more. Over time, alternative investments have become increasingly popular among investors looking for higher returns and diversification in their portfolios.

In the context of the Indian middle-class investor, alternatives offer a way to break free from the limitations of traditional investments. India's stock market can be volatile, and real estate prices can be high. By diversifying into alternatives, you can reduce risks and open doors to higher returns.

2. Why Alternatives are Gaining Popularity

Alternative investments typically offer higher potential returns than traditional options like FDs or savings accounts. However, they often come with higher risk. This chapter explores why alternatives are becoming a popular choice for savvy investors.

Rising Wealth of the Middle-Class: India's growing middle class is beginning to look beyond traditional forms of investment.

Low Interest Rates on FDs: As interest rates on FDs and savings accounts have declined, investors are looking for ways to grow their wealth faster.

Inflation: With inflation rising, investors are seeking ways to preserve their wealth and outpace the cost of living.

Alternative investments offer two main advantages:

Higher Potential Returns: Many alternatives provide returns that outpace traditional investments, making them attractive for wealth creation.

Diversification: Alternatives behave differently from traditional markets, reducing overall portfolio risk and shielding against volatility.

For the middle-class Indian investor, this chapter is about discovering alternative investments that align with your risk tolerance, financial goals, and cultural preferences.

3. Types of Alternative Investments

a. Real Estate Investment Trusts (REITs)

Real Estate Investment Trusts (REITs) allow individuals to invest in real estate without needing substantial capital. With REITs, you buy shares in a trust that owns and manages income-generating properties, such as office buildings, malls, and apartments.

Why consider REITs?

Provides regular income through dividends.

Offers diversification in the real estate sector with lower entry barriers than owning physical property.

Example: Indian REITs like Embassy Office Parks or Mindspace have shown steady growth.

b. Commodities

Commodities like gold, silver, crude oil, and agricultural products are long-standing alternatives for Indian investors. Gold, in particular, is ingrained in Indian culture as a store of value and hedge against inflation.

Other Commodities to Consider:

Silver: Often considered a cheaper alternative to gold, with industrial demand contributing to price stability.

Crude Oil: High-risk but rewarding for investors who understand global energy markets.

Agricultural Products: Wheat, coffee, and other agri-commodities offer opportunities to invest in India's backbone industry.

c. Invoice Discounting

What is it?

Invoice discounting is a form of short-term financing where businesses sell unpaid invoices at a discount to investors. Investors earn returns once the invoices are paid.

Why consider invoice discounting?

Low Risk: These are backed by confirmed invoices, so default risks are minimal.

Steady Returns: Investors can expect annualized returns ranging from 10% to 15%.

Short-Term Commitment: Ideal for those looking for liquidity, as invoice discounting typically involves durations of 30–90 days.

How to get started?

Platforms like KredX and TradeCred make it easy for individuals to invest in invoice discounting with small amounts.

d. Peer-to-Peer (P2P) Lending Platforms

What is it?

P2P lending platforms connect individual borrowers with investors willing to lend money for a fixed return.

Why is it growing in popularity?

Higher Returns: P2P lending offers returns of 8%-15%, much higher than traditional savings instruments.

Diversification: You can lend small amounts to multiple borrowers, spreading your risk.

Impact: It allows investors to contribute to the economy by providing credit to individuals and businesses.

Risks to consider:

Default risk is higher than traditional investments, so platforms like Faircent and Lendbox often grade borrowers based on creditworthiness.

e. Private Debt

What is it?

Private debt involves lending money to private companies, often through specialized funds. Unlike traditional bonds, private debt isn't traded on public markets.

Why consider private debt?

High Returns: With interest rates ranging from 10%-20%, private debt can be a lucrative option.

Flexibility: Offers customized investment terms depending on the company's needs.

Portfolio Balance: Provides stable returns, especially in times of stock market volatility.

Example in India: Startups and mid-sized businesses often raise private debt through platforms like CredAvenue.

f. Cryptocurrencies

What is it?

Cryptocurrencies are digital currencies like Bitcoin, Ethereum, and Solana that use blockchain technology.

Why invest in cryptocurrencies?

High Growth Potential: Cryptos have demonstrated exponential growth, albeit with significant volatility.

Diversification: Provides exposure to the rapidly growing blockchain ecosystem.

Risks to consider:

The Indian government is still clarifying regulations around cryptocurrencies, making this a high-risk investment for now.

g. Diversification: The Golden Rule of Alternatives

Diversification means spreading your investments across various asset classes to reduce overall risk. Alternative investments are especially valuable for diversification because they behave differently from traditional markets. For example:

When stocks perform poorly, commodities like gold often rise.

When real estate prices stagnate, P2P lending and invoice discounting can offer steady returns.

A well-diversified portfolio might include:

40% in equities or mutual funds.

20% in REITs and real estate investments.

10% in gold or other commodities.

10% in alternative debt options like invoice discounting and P2P lending.

20% in long-term alternatives like private equity or cryptocurrencies.

4. Why Alternatives Suit the Indian Middle-Class Investor

Higher Returns Than Traditional Avenues

With FDs offering sub-6% returns and inflation eating into those earnings, alternatives like P2P lending (8%-15%) and invoice discounting (10%-15%) provide a way to grow wealth meaningfully.

Access to New Opportunities

Platforms like KredX, Faircent, and CoinSwitch Kuber make it easy for Indians to access these investments. Many of these options now allow small-ticket entry points, making them accessible to the middle class.

Risk Management

Alternatives help reduce portfolio risk by ensuring you're not dependent on a single market or asset class. For instance, during the COVID-19 pandemic, gold prices surged while the stock market crashed—those who had diversified into gold saw their portfolios remain relatively stable.

5. Actionable Steps to Start Investing in Alternatives

Start Small: Begin with a fraction of your portfolio (e.g., 10%) in alternative investments.

Research Trusted Platforms: Explore platforms like KredX, Faircent, and Lendbox for low-risk options.

Consult Advisors: Speak to a financial advisor to align alternatives with your overall goals.

Regularly Review: Monitor your investments periodically and adjust based on market trends.

Alternative investments offer higher returns and diversification, making them an excellent option for middle-class investors in India.

Options like invoice discounting, P2P lending, and private debt are emerging as viable alternatives to FDs and savings accounts.

Diversification is crucial: Use alternatives to balance risk and optimize returns.

Start small, research well, and make informed decisions.

CHAPTER THREE

WHY ALTERNATIVES ARE UNDERVALUED

In the vast financial landscape, alternative investments have remained a lesser-explored avenue for many middle-class Indians. Despite their potential, misconceptions and myths have led to their undervaluation. In this chapter, we explore why alternative investments are often overlooked, dispel common myths, and highlight emerging trends that promise a bright future for this asset class.

1. Introduction: A Misunderstood Opportunity

Traditional investments like Fixed Deposits, mutual funds, and gold dominate Indian households. Alternatives, by comparison, are shrouded in skepticism due to their complexity and the perceived risks involved. However, these investments hold immense potential for those willing to dig deeper.

Why are they undervalued?

Lack of Awareness: Many investors are unfamiliar with alternative investment products like invoice discounting, private debt, or peer-to-peer lending.

Misconceptions About Risk: Alternatives are often seen as riskier than traditional investments, although this is not always true.

Limited Accessibility: Until recently, many alternative investments required high capital or institutional access, discouraging retail investors.

Let's explore and debunk these misconceptions.

2. Dispelling Myths and Misconceptions

Myth 1: "Alternatives Are Only for the Wealthy"

Traditionally, alternative investments were reserved for High Net-Worth Individuals (HNIs) and institutional investors. However, technology has democratized access.

Fact:

Platforms like Faircent, KredX, and GripInvest now allow investments as low as ₹5,000, making them accessible to the middle class.

Myth 2: "They're Too Risky"

Many equate alternatives with high risk due to lack of familiarity. However, the risk in alternative investments varies widely depending on the asset class. For instance:

Invoice Discounting: Low risk due to short durations and confirmed invoices.

Private Debt: Moderate risk with stable returns.

Cryptocurrencies: High risk but potentially high rewards.

Fact:

Proper diversification within alternatives can reduce portfolio volatility and enhance stability.

Myth 3: "Alternatives Lack Liquidity"

Liquidity is a concern for some alternative investments like private equity or real estate. However, several options, like P2P lending or invoice discounting, have short lock-in periods ranging from 30–90 days.

Fact:

Not all alternatives are illiquid. Options like REITs and invoice discounting offer relatively quick access to your funds.

Myth 4: "It's Too Complicated"

Complex terminology and lack of transparency deter many from exploring alternatives. However, modern platforms have simplified processes through user-friendly interfaces and educational resources.

Fact:

Platforms like Zerodha Varsity, Groww, and others now provide step-by-step guidance for alternative investment strategies.

3. Emerging Trends in Alternative Investments

a. Technology-Driven Platforms

The rise of fintech platforms is democratizing alternative investments. Apps and websites now provide access to fractional ownership, invoice discounting, and even private equity.

Example:

Platforms like TradeCred and GripInvest offer pre-vetted deals, making it easier for retail investors to participate in options that were once reserved for institutions.

b. Social and Impact Investing

Indian investors are increasingly looking at socially responsible investments. P2P lending and microfinance have emerged as a means to earn returns while contributing to society.

Example:

P2P platforms like Faircent allow investors to lend small amounts to individuals or small businesses, fostering financial inclusion.

c. Fractional Ownership

Fractional ownership lets investors buy a small percentage of high-value assets, such as real estate or high-end equipment.

Example:

Investors can now own a fraction of a commercial property through platforms like Strata with minimal upfront investment.

d. Rise of Green Investments

As sustainability becomes a global priority, green alternatives like renewable energy funds and carbon credit trading are gaining traction.

Example:

Renewable energy-focused funds in India offer exposure to the growing clean energy market.

e. Cryptocurrencies and Blockchain Technology

The crypto revolution is still unfolding in India, with the government introducing regulations to legitimize the sector. Blockchain applications beyond currency, such as tokenized assets and decentralized finance (DeFi), are poised for growth.

Example:

Platforms like WazirX and CoinSwitch Kuber are helping Indians explore cryptocurrency investments.

4. The Future Potential of Alternatives

a. Growing Middle-Class Appetite

India's growing middle class is becoming more financially savvy, with a rising interest in diversifying portfolios. The accessibility of alternatives is fueling this shift.

b. Regulatory Framework

The Indian government and SEBI are actively working to regulate alternative investment platforms, enhancing investor trust.

c. Integration with Traditional Portfolios

Financial advisors are increasingly incorporating alternatives into traditional portfolios to optimize risk-adjusted returns.

d. Digital Gold and Commodities

Digital gold and tokenized commodities are emerging as innovative ways to invest, making traditional alternatives like gold more accessible and liquid.

e. Wealth Creation Beyond Traditional Markets

With inflation outpacing the returns of traditional investments like FDs, alternatives are becoming a necessity rather than a luxury for achieving long-term wealth creation goals.

5. Action Plan: Tapping into the Potential

Educate Yourself: Understand the types of alternative investments and their risk profiles.

Start Small: Begin with low-ticket investments through trusted platforms to gain confidence.

Diversify: Allocate a portion of your portfolio to alternatives to balance risk and reward.

Stay Updated: Follow emerging trends and adjust your strategy as new opportunities arise.

Key Takeaways:

Alternative investments remain undervalued due to myths, misconceptions, and lack of awareness.

Fintech platforms and regulatory frameworks are making them more accessible to the middle class.

Emerging trends like fractional ownership, green investing, and digital commodities offer exciting opportunities for future growth.

With proper education and diversification, alternatives can unlock new wealth creation pathways for Indian investors.

CHAPTER FOUR

PRIVATE EQUITY AND VENTURE CAPITAL

Private Equity (PE) and Venture Capital (VC) are often viewed as exclusive investment realms dominated by institutional players and High Net Worth Individuals (HNIs). However, these private investment opportunities are increasingly accessible, even to small-scale investors. In this chapter, we'll demystify the world of PE and VC, explain how these investments work, and provide practical strategies for middle-class Indian investors looking to enter this exciting domain.

1. What Are Private Equity and Venture Capital?

Private Equity (PE):

Private equity involves investing directly in private companies or buying out public companies to restructure and improve their operations for long-term returns.

Key Features:

Focus on mature companies needing revitalization or growth capital.

Investments typically have a long-term horizon (5–10 years).

Returns are realized through dividends, interest, or selling stakes after value appreciation.

Venture Capital (VC):

Venture capital focuses on funding early-stage startups and high-growth companies. These investments carry higher risk but offer the potential for outsized returns.

Key Features:

Investments are in innovative, high-potential startups.

Returns are realized through Initial Public Offerings (IPOs) or mergers/acquisitions.

Typically involves smaller investment rounds with multiple participants.

Real-Life Example:

A VC firm like Sequoia Capital India funded startups such as Zomato and Byju's in their early stages, reaping massive returns after their success.

2. How Do Private Investments Work?

Private equity and venture capital investments follow a structured process:

Fundraising:

PE/VC firms pool funds from investors to create a fund.

Example: A   ₹100 crore PE fund may receive investments from individual investors, institutional investors, and family offices.

Investment Selection:

Firms identify potential companies for investment. For VC, this includes startups in sectors like fintech, edtech, or green energy. For PE, this involves established businesses needing a turnaround or growth capital.

Value Creation:

After investment, PE/VC firms actively work with the

management to improve operations, scale the business, or refine the business model.

Exit:

Returns are realized by selling the stake through an IPO, merger, or acquisition.

3. Strategies for Small-Scale Investors

a. Explore Alternate Routes

Middle-class investors may not have direct access to PE or VC funds but can explore:

Angel Investing Platforms: Platforms like AngelList India and LetsVenture enable small-ticket investments in early-stage startups.

Crowdfunding: Participating in equity crowdfunding campaigns on platforms like StartEngine or Tyke is another route.

Fractional Ownership Funds: Some funds now allow fractional ownership in private companies.

b. Choose Sector-Specific Opportunities

Focus on sectors with high growth potential, such as:

Green Energy: Investing in startups focused on renewable energy solutions.

Fintech: Companies disrupting traditional banking and financial services.

Healthtech: Startups innovating in telemedicine, diagnostics, and digital healthcare.

c. Start Small and Diversify

Allocate a small percentage (5–10%) of your portfolio to private investments.

Diversify across sectors and stages of businesses to balance risk and reward.

Example: Invest   ₹1,00,000 across five startups instead of putting it all in one.

d. Leverage Investment Syndicates

Joining syndicates allows smaller investors to collaborate with experienced investors or funds. Syndicates pool resources to make larger, collective investments.

Example: Indian Angel Network (IAN) allows smaller investors to participate in well-curated investment opportunities.

4. Benefits and Risks of Private Investments

Benefits:

High Returns Potential: VC and PE investments can deliver outsized returns compared to traditional markets.

Example: An early-stage investment in Flipkart delivered exponential returns to its investors after its acquisition by Walmart.

Portfolio Diversification: Adds uncorrelated assets to your portfolio, reducing dependence on stock market fluctuations.

Impact Investing: Many private investments support innovation and societal progress, aligning with personal values.

Risks:

High Risk of Failure: A majority of startups fail; only a few succeed spectacularly.

Illiquidity: Investments are locked for long periods, typically 5–10 years.

Lack of Transparency: Limited access to performance data or operational insights for small investors.

Mitigation Tip: Choose investments vetted by reputed platforms or syndicates, and focus on businesses with strong leadership and clear growth plans.

5. Emerging Trends in Private Equity and Venture Capital

a. Tech-Driven Access

Platforms like Tyke Invest and GrowX Ventures simplify PE and VC investing with minimal paperwork and transparent processes.

b. Focus on ESG (Environmental, Social, Governance)

Private funds increasingly prioritize companies that address environmental and social challenges, appealing to impact-conscious investors.

c. Domestic VC Ecosystem Boom

India's startup ecosystem is witnessing record-breaking growth, with homegrown funds focusing on local innovation.

d. Rise of Micro-VCs and Angel Syndicates

Micro-VC funds and angel syndicates are creating opportunities for smaller investors to enter the VC space with limited capital.

6. How to Get Started with Private Investments?

Educate Yourself: Gain knowledge about the PE/VC ecosystem through books, podcasts, and platforms like YourStory or Inc42.

Start Networking: Attend startup events, pitch sessions, or angel investor meetups in your city.

Use Fintech Platforms: Explore trusted platforms like Tyke and LetsVenture to begin small-ticket investments.

Consult Advisors: If unsure, consult financial advisors specializing in alternative investments.

Key Takeaways:

Private equity and venture capital provide high-growth investment opportunities previously inaccessible to middle-class investors.

Emerging platforms and syndicates are breaking barriers, making these investments more inclusive.

While risks are high, diversification, sector-specific focus, and networking can improve success rates.

India's growing startup ecosystem and tech-driven platforms offer significant potential for small-scale investors.

CHAPTER FIVE

REAL ESTATE BEYOND HOUSING

Real estate has long been a favorite asset class for Indian investors. Traditionally, it has been synonymous with buying land or residential properties. However, the world of real estate is far broader than just housing. From Real Estate Investment Trusts (REITs) to fractional ownership and commercial property investments, there are numerous opportunities for middle-class Indians to diversify their portfolios and gain exposure to real estate's potential without the high capital commitment of traditional purchases.

1. The Traditional Real Estate Mindset

Historically, Indian investors have favored land or housing as a means of wealth creation and security.

Perception: Real estate is a "safe" investment with steady appreciation.

Challenges:

High entry costs.

Long-term illiquidity.

Maintenance burdens.

Emerging Alternative: Modern real estate investments like REITs and fractional ownership eliminate these barriers, offering easy and cost-effective access to this asset class.

2. Real Estate Investment Trusts (REITs)

What Are REITs?

REITs are companies that own, operate, or finance income-generating real estate. They pool money from multiple investors to purchase and manage properties like office spaces, shopping malls, and warehouses.

How They Work:

Investors buy units of a REIT, similar to purchasing shares of a company.

REITs earn income from rent and property appreciation, which is shared as dividends.

Benefits of REITs for Indian Investors

Low Entry Costs: You can start with as little as ₹300–₹500 per unit.

Liquidity: REIT units are traded on stock exchanges, allowing investors to buy and sell easily.

Diversification: Gain exposure to high-value commercial properties without owning them outright.

Regular Income: SEBI mandates REITs to distribute 90% of their rental income as dividends.

Example:

REITs like Embassy Office Parks and Mindspace Business Parks have become popular among Indian investors for their stable returns.

3. Fractional Ownership

What Is Fractional Ownership?

Fractional ownership allows multiple investors to jointly own a property by pooling their resources.

Investors own a share of the property and receive a proportionate share of rental income.

Common in commercial real estate, such as office spaces, warehouses, and retail outlets.

How It Works:

A property worth ₹10 crore might be divided into 100 shares of ₹10 lakh each.

Investors buy shares based on their capacity.

Rental income is distributed monthly or quarterly based on ownership percentages.

Benefits:

Affordability: Own a slice of high-value commercial real estate without a large capital outlay.

Stable Income: Regular rental income from high-demand properties.

Professional Management: Properties are typically managed by experienced firms, reducing hassles.

Platforms Offering Fractional Ownership in India:

MyRE Capital

RealX

Example:

An investor with ₹5 lakh can participate in the ownership of a ₹5 crore Grade A office space and earn passive rental income.

4. Commercial Properties: A Lucrative Option

Why Invest in Commercial Real Estate?

Commercial properties, such as office spaces, retail outlets, and warehouses, offer higher rental yields (7–10%) compared to residential properties (2–3%).

Growing Demand: India's IT sector and e-commerce boom have increased demand for office spaces and warehouses.

Better Tenants: Corporates and businesses ensure regular, timely rent payments.

Longer Lease Periods: Commercial leases typically last for 5–10 years, providing stability.

How Middle-Class Investors Can Participate:

REITs and Fractional Ownership: As mentioned above, these allow indirect exposure.

Co-Working Spaces: Investing in co-working hubs like WeWork or Awfis properties is an emerging trend.

Industrial Real Estate: Warehouses and logistics parks are gaining traction due to the e-commerce boom.

5. Key Trends Shaping the Future of Real Estate Investments

a. Digital Platforms for Real Estate Investing

Fintech platforms have made real estate investments more accessible, allowing investors to browse properties, track income, and manage investments online.

b. Smart Cities and Urban Expansion

Government initiatives like Smart Cities and affordable housing schemes are increasing the scope of real estate investment opportunities.

c. ESG-Driven Real Estate

Investors are prioritizing green buildings and energy-efficient properties for their environmental and financial benefits.

d. The Post-Pandemic Commercial Boom

As hybrid work models stabilize, demand for Grade A office spaces and flexible leasing terms is increasing.

6. Risks to Consider

a. Market Volatility:

Rental yields and property values are influenced by economic conditions and tenant stability.

b. Illiquidity:

Even with fractional ownership, selling your stake may not always be quick or easy.

c. Management Fees:

Platforms managing fractional ownership properties charge fees, which could impact net returns.

d. Tenant Dependency:

Vacancies or non-performing tenants can disrupt income streams.

Mitigation Tip: Invest in REITs or platforms with a proven track record of managing high-occupancy properties.

7. Getting Started with Real Estate Beyond Housing

Research REITs: Start by exploring Indian REITs like Embassy Office Parks, which are listed on the NSE.

Try Fractional Ownership: Use platforms like RealX to invest small amounts in premium commercial properties.

Focus on Diversification: Allocate a portion of your portfolio to real estate while balancing it with other asset classes like equities and mutual funds.

Seek Expert Advice: Consult real estate advisors or use platforms offering detailed analytics to make informed decisions.

Key Takeaways:

Real estate investment is no longer limited to housing; REITs, fractional ownership, and commercial properties open doors for middle-class investors.

With lower entry costs and professional management, modern real estate options are more accessible and scalable.

Though risks exist, careful research and diversification can mitigate them while offering stable returns.

Platforms and government initiatives are driving innovation in real estate investment opportunities for Indians.

CHAPTER SIX

COMMODITIES AND PRECIOUS METALS

Diversification through Gold, Silver, and Beyond

For centuries, commodities like gold and silver have been trusted as stores of value and safe havens during economic uncertainty. Today, with a dynamic global economy and changing investment landscapes, commodities are no longer limited to precious metals—they now include energy resources, agricultural products, and even water. For middle-class Indian investors, understanding these assets is critical to achieving diversification and stability in their investment portfolios.

1. Why Commodities Matter for Diversification

Commodities are physical assets that serve as a hedge against inflation, currency devaluation, and economic downturns. Unlike stocks or bonds, their value is tied to tangible goods, making them less vulnerable to market sentiment.

Advantages of Investing in Commodities:

Hedge Against Inflation: Commodity prices often rise when inflation increases, protecting purchasing power.

Portfolio Diversification: Commodities have low correlation with traditional asset classes like equities.

Global Demand: Industrial growth, especially in emerging economies like India, ensures steady demand for resources like metals and energy.

2. Gold: The Timeless Asset

Why Gold Stands Out

Gold is deeply ingrained in Indian culture, symbolizing wealth, prosperity, and security. From jewelry to bars and coins, it's a preferred investment avenue for middle-class families.

Store of Value: Gold retains value over time, making it a reliable long-term investment.

Crisis Shield: During economic or geopolitical crises, gold prices tend to rise, offering stability.

Liquidity: Gold is highly liquid; it can be sold or exchanged for cash almost instantly.

Ways to Invest in Gold:

Physical Gold: Jewelry, bars, or coins are traditional options but come with storage and security challenges.

Gold ETFs: Exchange-traded funds allow investors to gain exposure to gold without owning it physically.

Sovereign Gold Bonds (SGBs): Issued by the Government of India, these bonds offer periodic interest and eliminate the need for storage.

Digital Gold: Platforms like Paytm and PhonePe allow investors to buy small amounts of gold online, starting from as low as   ₹1.

3. Silver: The Affordable Cousin

Silver is often called the "poor man's gold," but its importance in the industrial and technological sectors gives it unique value.

Key Benefits of Silver:

Industrial Demand: Used in electronics, solar panels, and medical devices.

Lower Entry Point: Silver is more affordable than gold, making it accessible for small investors.

Potential for Growth: With the rise of renewable energy, silver's industrial use is expected to grow.

How to Invest in Silver:

Physical Silver: Like gold, silver can be purchased in the form of coins, bars, or jewelry.

Silver ETFs and Futures: These allow investors to trade in silver without physical possession.

4. Beyond Precious Metals: Expanding into Other Commodities

a. Energy Commodities

Crude Oil and Natural Gas: Vital for global energy needs, these commodities can be invested in through futures or commodity-focused mutual funds.

Renewable Energy Resources: Emerging options like lithium (used in EV batteries) and carbon credits are gaining attention.

b. Agricultural Commodities

Grains: Wheat, rice, and corn are staples with consistent demand.

Edible Oils: Commodities like palm oil and soybean oil are key components of the Indian diet and market.

Sugar and Spices: With India being a leading producer, these offer unique opportunities.

c. Other Precious Commodities

Platinum and Palladium: Used in industrial applications like catalytic converters, these metals are becoming attractive alternatives.

5. Risks and Challenges in Commodities Investing
Market Volatility
Commodity prices are often affected by unpredictable factors like weather, geopolitical events, and global demand-supply imbalances.
Storage and Security:
For physical assets like gold or silver, safe storage is essential but can be costly.
Leverage Risk:
Commodities trading, especially in futures, often involves leverage, which can amplify losses.
Regulatory Hurdles:
Taxation policies and restrictions on certain commodities may pose barriers to small investors.
6. Strategies for Middle-Class Investors
Start with Familiar Assets: Begin with gold or silver, as these are widely understood and culturally accepted.
Diversify Gradually: Once comfortable, explore agricultural and energy commodities through mutual funds or ETFs.
Use SIPs for Gold: Systematic Investment Plans (SIPs) in gold ETFs or SGBs can make investing affordable and consistent.
Stay Informed: Keep track of global trends, government policies, and market dynamics affecting commodity prices.
Set Clear Goals: Define whether you're looking for long-term wealth preservation (gold) or short-term gains (energy or agricultural commodities).
7. The Future of Commodities Investing
Digital Commodities
With advancements in blockchain technology, tokenized commodities are emerging, allowing fractional ownership of assets like gold, oil, or even agricultural

produce.

Green Commodities

As the world moves towards sustainability, commodities linked to renewable energy and environmental initiatives are expected to gain prominence.

India's Growing Role

As India continues its economic growth, demand for commodities like gold, silver, oil, and agricultural produce will likely increase, creating more opportunities for investors.

Key Takeaways:

Commodities, led by gold and silver, provide an excellent hedge against inflation and economic uncertainty.

Diversification into energy, agriculture, and industrial metals can enhance portfolio stability.

With options like ETFs, SGBs, and digital gold, investing in commodities has become accessible to middle-class Indians.

A well-informed, gradual approach can help investors tap into the full potential of commodities while mitigating risks.

CHAPTER SEVEN

COLLECTIBLES AND PASSION INVESTMENTS

Art, Wine, Rare Books, and Cars—How to Invest Smartly

Investing in collectibles and passion assets is as much about personal interest as it is about financial gain. Whether it's a rare painting, a vintage car, or an antique book, these investments combine emotional satisfaction with the potential for wealth creation. For middle-class Indian investors, this chapter sheds light on how to approach passion investments strategically and turn hobbies into lucrative opportunities.

1. What Are Collectibles and Passion Investments?

Collectibles are physical items that hold cultural, historical, or aesthetic value, while passion investments include assets driven by personal interest, such as fine art or luxury goods. These are unique, tangible investments whose value often appreciates over time due to rarity, demand, and provenance.

Examples of Collectibles and Passion Investments:

Art - Paintings, sculptures, or photographs by renowned artists.

Wine and Spirits - Limited-edition bottles or vintage wines.

Rare Books and Manuscripts - First editions, signed copies, or historic texts.

Classic and Vintage Cars - Automobiles with historical or cultural significance.

Stamps and Coins - Philately and numismatics as traditional passion investments.

Memorabilia - Sports gear, celebrity items, or cultural artifacts.

2. Why Consider Collectibles?

a. Diversification

Collectibles offer a non-correlated asset class that can stabilize portfolios during stock market downturns.

b. Cultural and Emotional Value

Many collectibles hold sentimental value and allow investors to blend passion with purpose.

c. Potential for High Returns

Some items, like rare paintings or vintage cars, have seen exponential appreciation over decades.

d. Status Symbol

Owning high-value collectibles often signals prestige and taste, making them aspirational for many middle-class families.

3. The Challenges of Investing in Collectibles

a. Illiquidity

Selling collectibles can take time, as they require niche buyers willing to pay a premium.

b. Expertise Required

Understanding authenticity, provenance, and market trends demands specialized knowledge.

c. Maintenance and Storage

Items like art or cars need proper care, which can be expensive.

d. Market Volatility

Prices for passion investments can fluctuate widely due to changing tastes or economic conditions.

4. Investing in Art: Creativity Meets Capital

What to Look For:

Renowned Artists: Works by established Indian artists like MF Husain, Raja Ravi Varma, or modern-day talents.

Emerging Artists: Investing early in promising artists can yield significant returns.

Authenticity: Ensure the artwork is genuine and accompanied by proper documentation.

How to Start:

Online Platforms: Websites like Saffronart or Astaguru allow bidding on Indian art.

Local Galleries: Attend exhibitions to discover both established and upcoming artists.

Art Funds: Pool resources with other investors to own high-value artworks collectively.

5. Wine and Spirits: Sipping Profits

Why Invest in Wine and Spirits?

Rare wines and limited-edition bottles can appreciate in value while offering the option of personal enjoyment.

India's growing wine culture and emerging brands like Sula and Fratelli offer opportunities for small-scale investors.

Key Strategies:

Understand Vintage Value: Older vintages from reputed vineyards tend to appreciate.

Proper Storage: Ensure wines are stored in climate-controlled environments to preserve quality.

Online Marketplaces: Platforms like Liv-ex connect investors with global fine wine markets.

6. Rare Books and Manuscripts: Turning Pages into Profits

Books are timeless investments that combine history, culture, and financial potential.

What to Look For:

First Editions: Original prints of famous works hold significant value.

Signed Copies: Autographed books by authors add uniqueness.

Cultural Importance: Books tied to Indian history, such as first editions of Gandhian writings, are highly sought after.

How to Get Started:

Explore online auction sites like Christie's or local rare book dealers.

Check personal libraries or second-hand bookstores for hidden gems.

7. Classic Cars: Nostalgia on Wheels

Why Invest in Vintage Cars?

Classic cars appreciate in value over time, especially limited-production models.

Brands like Rolls-Royce, Jaguar, or vintage Marutis hold cultural and collector appeal.

Things to Keep in Mind:

Condition and Authenticity: Original parts and good maintenance boost value.

Market Trends: Understand which brands or models are currently sought after.

Restoration Costs: Factor in expenses for repairing or maintaining vintage cars.

8. Starting Small: Tips for Middle-Class Investors

Identify Your Passion: Choose a category you love and understand.

Set a Budget: Start with affordable items and gradually scale investments.

Research Thoroughly: Attend auctions, visit galleries, or join collector groups to learn market trends.

Use Online Platforms: Leverage technology to access collectibles and passion investments globally.

Seek Expert Advice: Consult professionals to verify authenticity and assess value.

9. The Future of Collectibles and Passion Investments in India

Digital Collectibles: With the rise of blockchain, NFTs (non-fungible tokens) are revolutionizing how art, music, and even memes are owned and traded.

Cultural Preservation: India's rich heritage offers vast opportunities in traditional collectibles like temple artifacts or tribal art.

Growing Middle-Class Interest: As disposable incomes rise, collectibles are becoming a viable asset class for more Indians.

Collectibles blend emotional satisfaction with financial returns, offering a unique diversification opportunity.

From art to vintage cars, each category demands passion, patience, and knowledge.

Middle-class investors can start small, focusing on categories they understand and appreciate.

With proper care, research, and market awareness, passion investments can evolve into a profitable hobby.

CHAPTER EIGHT

RISK VS. REWARD IN ALTERNATIVES

Assessing Liquidity, Volatility, and Time Horizons

Investing in alternative assets can offer lucrative rewards, but it comes with its own set of risks. This chapter focuses on understanding these risks and balancing them against potential returns. It provides practical advice for middle-class Indian investors to make informed decisions while navigating the complexities of alternative investments.

1. Understanding the Risk-Reward Relationship

In finance, risk and reward are directly proportional—the higher the potential return, the greater the risk. Alternative investments often provide non-traditional growth opportunities, but they require a deeper understanding of the associated risks to achieve sustainable returns.

Key Factors to Consider:

Liquidity: Ease of converting the investment into cash.

Volatility: Degree of price fluctuation over a period.

Time Horizon: The duration for which capital is tied up.

2. Common Risks in Alternative Investments

a. Liquidity Risk

Unlike stocks or mutual funds, many alternative assets are not easily liquidated. For instance, private equity or real estate investments often require long-term commitments.

Example: Fractional ownership in real estate may take months or years to sell.

Mitigation Tip: Allocate only a portion of your portfolio to illiquid assets.

b. Volatility Risk

Some alternatives, like cryptocurrencies and commodities, experience significant price fluctuations due to market dynamics.

Example: Bitcoin prices can swing by double-digit percentages in a single day.

Mitigation Tip: Limit exposure to volatile assets and diversify across stable alternatives.

c. Market Risk

Changes in economic policies, inflation, or geopolitical tensions can impact the performance of alternative investments.

Example: Rising interest rates can reduce the profitability of REITs.

Mitigation Tip: Stay updated on macroeconomic trends and adjust your portfolio accordingly.

d. Regulatory Risk

Governments may introduce new regulations that affect alternative investments.

Example: Tax policies on gold imports in India can impact returns on precious metal investments.

Mitigation Tip: Consult financial advisors to understand the regulatory environment.

e. Management Risk

For investments like private equity or peer-to-peer lending, the success largely depends on the management team or platform.

Example: A poorly managed startup funded through venture capital may fail.

Mitigation Tip: Conduct due diligence on the leadership and track records before investing.

3. Evaluating Rewards of Alternative Investments

Despite the risks, alternatives can provide substantial benefits, such as:

a. High Returns

Some alternatives, like private equity or cryptocurrency, have the potential for exponential growth.

b. Diversification

Alternatives often behave differently from traditional assets, reducing portfolio risk during market downturns.

c. Inflation Hedge

Assets like gold or real estate can act as a hedge against inflation, preserving your purchasing power.

d. Unique Opportunities

Investments in art, wine, or rare collectibles offer tangible assets and emotional satisfaction.

4. Balancing Liquidity, Volatility, and Time Horizons

a. Liquidity Assessment

Short-Term Goals: Focus on liquid assets like REITs or publicly traded alternatives.

Long-Term Goals: Consider illiquid options like private equity or real estate for growth over time.

b. Volatility Management

Allocate no more than 20-30% of your portfolio to highly volatile assets like cryptocurrencies or commodities.

Diversify with stable alternatives, such as debt funds or microfinance.

c. Aligning with Time Horizons

Short-Term Investors (1-3 Years): Peer-to-peer lending or invoice discounting.

Medium-Term Investors (3-7 Years): Commodities, REITs, or fractional ownership.

Long-Term Investors (7+ Years): Venture capital, private equity, or farmland investments.

5. Tools and Strategies for Risk Assessment

a. Diversification

Spreading investments across multiple asset classes reduces the impact of a single asset's underperformance.

b. Risk Tolerance Assessment

Understand your financial goals and emotional capacity to handle losses. Tools like risk profiling questionnaires can help.

c. Monitoring and Rebalancing

Regularly review your portfolio and make adjustments to align with market conditions.

d. Seeking Expert Advice

Financial advisors or online platforms can provide insights into emerging trends and risks.

6. Real-Life Example: A Balanced Portfolio

Investor Profile:

Name: Arjun, 35 years old, software professional.

Monthly Income: ₹1,50,000

Investment Goals: Wealth creation for retirement (20 years) and children's education (10 years).

Portfolio Allocation:

40% in traditional investments: Mutual funds, stocks, and FDs.

30% in alternatives:

10% in REITs (income-generating properties).

10% in gold ETFs (inflation hedge).

5% in private debt (stable returns).

5% in cryptocurrencies (high risk, high reward).

30% in savings and emergency funds.

Key Takeaways:

Alternative investments offer unique growth opportunities but come with specific risks.

Evaluate your liquidity needs, risk tolerance, and time horizon before investing.

Diversify across multiple asset classes to minimize overall risk.

Stay informed about market trends, economic conditions, and regulatory changes.

Start small, monitor performance, and adjust your strategy as you gain experience.

CHAPTER NINE

STARTING SMALL: ENTRY POINTS FOR BEGINNERS

Platforms and Tools to Get Started

For middle-class Indian investors, the world of alternative investments may seem intimidating at first. However, starting small with accessible platforms and tools can simplify the process and build confidence. This chapter focuses on practical entry points, affordable options, and beginner-friendly strategies to explore alternative investments.

1. Why Start Small?

a. Low Initial Risk

Beginning with small investments allows you to test the waters without risking a significant portion of your savings.

b. Learning Curve

Understanding how alternative investments work takes time. Starting small provides hands-on experience while minimizing potential mistakes.

c. Portfolio Flexibility

Smaller investments enable better diversification, making it easier to balance risks and rewards across different asset classes.

2. Beginner-Friendly Alternative Investment Options

**a. Peer-to-Peer Lending Platforms

P2P platforms connect borrowers with individual lenders, offering returns typically higher than traditional savings accounts.

Platforms in India: Faircent, LenDenClub, and RupeeCircle.

Minimum Investment: ₹500 - ₹5,000 per loan.

Pro Tip: Diversify across multiple borrowers to mitigate default risks.

**b. Invoice Discounting

This involves investing in unpaid invoices of businesses and earning returns when clients settle their bills.

Platforms in India: KredX, TradeCred.

Minimum Investment: ₹10,000 per invoice.

Pro Tip: Choose invoices backed by reputed companies to reduce risk.

c. Real Estate Investment Trusts (REITs)

REITs allow you to invest in commercial properties without the need for large capital.

Listed REITs in India: Embassy Office Parks REIT, Mindspace Business Parks REIT.

Minimum Investment: ₹300 - ₹500 (price of one share).

Pro Tip: Focus on dividend-paying REITs for steady income.

d. Gold ETFs and Digital Gold

Gold remains a popular investment among Indian households. Digital gold and ETFs offer a modern way to invest without the hassle of physical storage.

Platforms: Paytm Gold, Groww, and Zerodha.

Minimum Investment: As low as ₹100.

Pro Tip: Use gold as a hedge against inflation, not for short-term gains.

e. Fractional Ownership

Platforms enable you to own a fraction of high-value assets like real estate or art.

Platforms in India: hBits, Strata.

Minimum Investment: ₹10,000 - ₹25,000.

Pro Tip: Research property locations and expected rental yields before investing.

f. Cryptocurrency Exchanges

Cryptocurrencies like Bitcoin and Ethereum provide high-risk, high-reward opportunities.

Platforms in India: CoinDCX, WazirX, ZebPay.

Minimum Investment: As low as ₹100.

Pro Tip: Invest only what you can afford to lose and focus on blue-chip cryptocurrencies.

3. Tools and Resources for Beginners

a. Investment Apps

User-friendly apps simplify investing by offering detailed analytics and automated tracking.

Popular Apps: Zerodha (for REITs), CRED Mint (for lending), and Paytm (for gold).

b. Online Learning Platforms

Educate yourself before diving into alternative investments.

Options: Coursera, Udemy, and YouTube channels like "Kaliyug Kuber."

c. Financial Calculators

Tools like SIP calculators, loan EMI calculators, and portfolio trackers help you plan your investments effectively.

d. Communities and Forums

Join investment groups on platforms like Reddit, Telegram, or local WhatsApp groups to exchange knowledge and strategies.

4. Key Tips for Getting Started

a. Set Clear Goals

Define what you want to achieve: steady income, capital appreciation, or portfolio diversification.

b. Start with What You Know

Choose assets you understand, such as gold or P2P lending, before exploring complex options like cryptocurrencies.

c. Invest Regularly

Use SIP (Systematic Investment Plan) options where available to build a portfolio gradually.

d. Stay Disciplined

Avoid impulsive decisions based on market trends or peer pressure. Stick to your financial plan.

e. Monitor and Learn

Track the performance of your investments and analyze what works and what doesn't.

5. Case Study: Ramesh's First Steps in Alternative Investments

Background:

Ramesh, a 32-year-old schoolteacher in Hyderabad, wanted to explore alternative investments to supplement his income.

Initial Steps:

Invested ₹5,000 in P2P lending on Faircent.

Bought gold worth ₹2,000 digitally through Paytm.

Allocated ₹1,000 monthly for a SIP in a gold ETF on Zerodha.

Outcome After 1 Year:

P2P lending generated an annual return of 10%.

Gold appreciated by 8%, acting as a hedge against inflation.

Ramesh gained confidence to diversify further into REITs.

6. Common Mistakes to Avoid

Overcommitting Capital: Start small to minimize losses.

Ignoring Research: Lack of due diligence can lead to poor investment decisions.

Chasing High Returns: Focus on stable, consistent growth rather than quick profits.

Neglecting Diversification: Spreading investments reduces overall risk.

7. Starting Small: The Path to Financial Growth

Alternative investments provide middle-class Indians with an opportunity to break free from traditional financial products. With a small initial commitment, patience, and continued learning, you can create a diverse portfolio that balances risk and reward effectively.

CHAPTER TEN

BLENDING TRADITIONAL AND ALTERNATIVE INVESTMENTS

Crafting a Balanced, Resilient Portfolio

The secret to long-term financial success lies in striking a balance between traditional and alternative investments. While traditional investments offer stability and steady growth, alternative investments provide diversification and opportunities for higher returns. This chapter guides Indian middle-class investors on how to blend both effectively to build a resilient portfolio.

1. The Importance of Diversification

a. Spreading Risk

By investing in multiple asset classes, you can minimize the impact of poor performance in one area.

b. Enhancing Returns

Alternative investments often have low correlation with traditional assets, which means they can perform well even when stocks or bonds struggle.

c. Resilience Against Inflation

Assets like gold, real estate, and commodities often act as a hedge against inflation, protecting your purchasing power.

2. Traditional vs. Alternative Investments: A Quick Comparison

3. Crafting a Balanced Portfolio

a. Determine Your Goals

Ask yourself:

Are you looking for steady income, capital appreciation, or wealth preservation?

What is your risk tolerance?

b. Allocate Based on Risk Tolerance

Conservative Investors (Low Risk):

70% in traditional investments (FDs, PPF, bonds).

30% in alternatives (gold, REITs, P2P lending).

Moderate Investors (Balanced Risk):

50% in traditional investments.

50% in alternatives (real estate, gold ETFs, invoice discounting).

Aggressive Investors (High Risk):

30% in traditional investments.

70% in alternatives (cryptocurrency, venture capital, private equity).

c. Monitor and Adjust

Periodically review your portfolio to ensure it aligns with your financial goals and market conditions.

4. Tools to Achieve Balance

a. SIPs (Systematic Investment Plans)

SIPs in mutual funds or ETFs allow you to invest in small amounts regularly, balancing your exposure to traditional markets.

b. Asset Allocation Platforms

Online tools like Zerodha, Groww, or INDmoney can guide your asset allocation across traditional and alternative investments.

c. Professional Guidance

Financial advisors can tailor a portfolio based on your income, expenses, and long-term goals.

5. Case Study: Blending Traditional and Alternative Investments

Profile:

Sunita, a 35-year-old working professional from Chennai, wanted to prepare for her children's education and her retirement.

Portfolio Allocation:

40% in traditional instruments:

PPF (₹3 lakhs/year).

Fixed Deposits (₹1.5 lakhs/year).

40% in mutual funds:

Equity and hybrid funds via SIP (₹20,000/month).

20% in alternatives:

REITs (₹50,000/year).

Digital gold (₹20,000/year).

Peer-to-peer lending (₹10,000/year).

Outcome After 5 Years:

Sunita's portfolio achieved steady growth while diversifying her risk, enabling her to confidently fund her children's education and plan for retirement.

6. Tips for Blending Traditional and Alternatives

a. Start With What You Know

Invest in familiar assets before exploring alternatives. For instance, begin with gold ETFs if you're unsure about P2P lending.

b. Maintain Liquidity

Ensure part of your portfolio is easily accessible for emergencies. Fixed deposits or short-term mutual funds can serve this purpose.

c. Reinvest Returns

Use the returns from traditional investments to fund alternative ventures, compounding your wealth over time.

d. Stay Informed

Keep up with market trends and emerging alternative options. Platforms like your own "Kaliyug Kuber" channel can provide valuable insights.

7. Blending in Practice: A Checklist for Success

Analyze Your Financial Goals – Short-term and long-term objectives.

Calculate Risk Tolerance – Are you comfortable with high-risk, high-reward scenarios?

Choose a Balanced Mix – Allocate assets proportionally based on your risk profile.

Review Regularly – Market conditions change; your portfolio should adapt.

Stay Consistent – Stick to your investment plan and avoid impulsive decisions.

8. The Balanced Portfolio: A Path to Financial Freedom

Blending traditional and alternative investments offers the best of both worlds—stability and growth potential. By carefully planning and diversifying, middle-class Indian investors can build a resilient portfolio that withstands market fluctuations and secures financial independence.

CHAPTER ELEVEN

ECONOMIC TRENDS SHAPING ALTERNATIVES

Inflation, Globalization, and Technology's Impact

The world of alternative investments does not operate in a vacuum. Global economic trends play a significant role in shaping the potential risks and rewards of these assets. This chapter examines three key factors—inflation, globalization, and technological advancements—and their impact on the growth and evolution of alternative investments, with a focus on the Indian middle-class perspective.

1. Inflation: A Double-Edged Sword

a. Understanding Inflation's Impact

Inflation erodes the purchasing power of money, making it essential for investors to seek assets that grow in value faster than inflation.

Impact on Alternatives:

Gold and Precious Metals: Gold is a traditional hedge against inflation, as its value tends to rise when inflation increases.

Real Estate: Property values and rental income often keep pace with or exceed inflation, offering protection against rising costs.

Cryptocurrencies: Though highly volatile, some see cryptocurrencies like Bitcoin as a hedge against fiat currency inflation.

Example:

During the post-pandemic inflation surge, gold prices in India surged from   ₹40,000 to   ₹60,000 per 10 grams within three years, making it a safe haven for many investors.

b. Inflation's Challenges for Investors

Increased Costs: Alternatives like real estate and collectibles may become more expensive to acquire and maintain.

Eroded Returns: Fixed-income alternatives like peer-to-peer lending may struggle to outpace inflation.

Strategies to Mitigate Inflation Risks:

Diversify into inflation-resistant assets like gold and REITs.

Consider variable-income alternatives like private equity, which offer the potential for higher returns.

2. Globalization: Bridging Markets

a. Access to Global Opportunities

Globalization has opened doors for Indian investors to explore alternative markets worldwide.

Examples of Global Alternatives:

International Real Estate: Fractional ownership in properties abroad.

Foreign Private Equity: Startups in Silicon Valley or Southeast Asia.

Art and Collectibles: Online platforms enabling investments in global art and wine markets.

b. Risks of Globalization

Currency Fluctuations: Investments in global assets are exposed to forex risks.

Regulatory Challenges: Each country has its own rules for taxation and ownership.

How to Navigate:

Use platforms that simplify international investments, such as WazirX (crypto) or YieldStreet (global alternatives).

Start with low-exposure investments like ETFs tied to global commodities or markets.

c. Globalization's Role in India

India's integration into global markets has brought innovations like fractional real estate and invoice discounting to the forefront, making alternative investments more accessible to middle-class investors.

3. Technology: A Game-Changer for Alternatives

a. Democratizing Access

Technology has revolutionized how investors participate in alternative markets:

Platforms: Apps like Groww and INDmoney bring private equity and P2P lending to your fingertips.

Blockchain: Enables fractional ownership of high-value assets like real estate or art through tokenization.

Case Study:

Raj, a 30-year-old from Hyderabad, used a P2P lending app to earn 12% annual returns by lending small amounts to verified borrowers, diversifying his income streams.

b. Enhanced Transparency

Blockchain ensures secure, tamper-proof records of transactions, building trust in alternatives like cryptocurrencies and tokenized assets.

c. Emerging Digital Trends

AI-Powered Insights: Tools using AI to predict trends in alternative markets.

Virtual Assets: The rise of NFTs as investment vehicles.

Crowdfunding: Platforms allowing individuals to invest in startups and niche markets with minimal capital.

4. Navigating Economic Trends: A Practical Guide

a. For Inflation-Resistant Investments

Allocate at least 20% of your portfolio to assets like gold, REITs, or commodities.

Avoid locking capital in low-yield alternatives during high inflation periods.

b. Leveraging Globalization

Start with globally recognized platforms offering fractional ownership or international exposure.

Diversify across countries and asset classes to reduce risks from any single economy.

c. Embracing Technology

Explore apps and blockchain-based platforms to streamline your investment journey.

Stay informed about emerging tech-driven alternatives like tokenized real estate or NFTs.

5. The Future of Alternatives in India

a. Rising Awareness

Indian investors are increasingly aware of the potential in alternatives, driven by accessible technology and global trends.

b. The Role of Young Investors

Tech-savvy millennials are leading the shift toward assets like cryptocurrencies and P2P lending, making these mainstream.

c. Policy and Regulation

As the government tightens regulations, especially for cryptocurrencies and P2P lending, alternatives will become safer and more structured.

Riding the Wave of Economic Trends

Understanding how inflation, globalization, and technology influence alternative investments can empower you to make smarter financial decisions. By aligning your portfolio with these trends, you can not only safeguard your wealth but also capitalize on emerging opportunities, ensuring a prosperous financial future.

CHAPTER TWELVE

CTRL+ALT: PLANNING FOR LONG-TERM WEALTH

Strategies for Legacy Creation and Financial Independence

Building long-term wealth is not just about accumulating assets—it's about creating a sustainable legacy and achieving financial independence. For Indian middle-class families, this involves planning investments that grow over time, ensuring financial security for future generations, and leveraging alternative investments as a cornerstone for wealth creation.

1. The Importance of Long-Term Wealth Planning

a. Securing Financial Independence

Financial independence means having enough assets to cover your expenses without relying on active income.

Key Goals:

Cover rising costs due to inflation.

Fund major life events like education, weddings, or retirement.

Leave a financial legacy for your children.

b. Legacy Creation: Beyond Wealth

Legacy isn't just about passing down money—it's about leaving behind a structured plan for your family's future.

Why Alternatives Matter:

They provide diversification and steady growth.

They offer protection against economic fluctuations.

2. Key Strategies for Long-Term Wealth Creation

a. Diversify with Alternatives

Traditional assets like fixed deposits or mutual funds may not always offer high returns. Diversifying into alternatives can unlock greater growth potential.

Examples:

Real Estate: Fractional ownership ensures steady rental income without high capital investment.

Private Debt: Offers fixed income with higher returns than traditional debt instruments.

Gold and Precious Metals: Serves as a safety net during market downturns.

Actionable Tip:

Allocate 25-30% of your portfolio to alternatives for steady growth and inflation protection.

b. Compounding and Reinvestment

Reinvesting earnings from alternatives like peer-to-peer lending or REIT dividends accelerates wealth accumulation.

The Rule of 72:

This simple formula helps estimate how quickly your investments will double. For instance, at a 10% annual return, your money doubles in approximately 7.2 years.

c. Tax-Efficient Planning

Taxes can erode your returns significantly. Invest in tax-efficient alternatives like REITs or government-approved bonds to minimize liabilities.

India-Specific Tips:

Invest in Sovereign Gold Bonds (SGBs) to earn interest and enjoy tax-free maturity returns.

Use the capital gains exemptions under Section 54EC for real estate profits.

3. Planning for Generational Wealth

a. Create a Wealth Transfer Plan

In India, succession planning often gets neglected. Structured planning ensures your family inherits your assets without unnecessary disputes.

Steps:

Draft a will specifying the distribution of alternative investments.

Explore creating a family trust to protect and grow wealth over generations.

Nominate beneficiaries for all investments to avoid legal hassles.

b. Invest in Education and Skills

One of the best ways to leave a legacy is by funding education or skill-building for the next generation, enabling them to sustain wealth independently.

4. Tools and Platforms for Wealth Planning

a. Wealth Management Platforms

Technology makes wealth planning accessible to middle-class investors.

INDmoney: Tracks investments across categories, including alternatives.

Groww: Allows easy investment in REITs, gold, and mutual funds.

Zerodha Varsity: Offers free education on advanced investment strategies.

b. Professional Advisors

Seek expert guidance for creating a comprehensive wealth management plan that includes alternatives.

5. Overcoming Challenges

a. Managing Volatility

Alternative investments can be volatile, especially cryptocurrencies or collectibles. Invest only what you can afford to lock away for the long term.

b. Staying Informed

Regularly monitor market trends and economic changes that could affect your alternative portfolio.

Example:

In 2020, the rise of REITs in India provided new avenues for wealth creation. Keeping informed about such trends enables timely action.

6. Ctrl+Alt: Unlocking Long-Term Wealth

The combination of control (Ctrl) and alternative investments (Alt) offers a powerful strategy for long-term wealth planning. Here's how:

Control: Maintain oversight of your portfolio through regular reviews and adjustments.

Alternatives: Use innovative assets to diversify, protect, and grow wealth.

7. Building a Roadmap to Financial Independence

Start Early: Time is your greatest ally in wealth creation. Begin small but start now.

Set Clear Goals: Define milestones, such as retirement savings or children's education funds.

Revisit Plans Regularly: Adjust allocations to align with life changes or market conditions.

8. Inspiring Success Story: The Naidu Family from Hyderabad

The Naidu family invested ₹50,000 annually in Sovereign Gold Bonds and REITs for 15 years. By reinvesting returns and maintaining discipline, they built a portfolio worth ₹50 lakh, ensuring their daughter's education and a stress-free retirement.

Conclusion: Achieving Financial Freedom

Long-term wealth creation is about crafting a sustainable strategy that aligns with your life goals. With alternative investments playing a pivotal role, financial independence is no longer a dream but an achievable reality.

CHAPTER THIRTEEN

INVOICE DISCOUNTING: UNLOCKING IMMEDIATE

Liquidity

Invoice discounting is an emerging alternative investment in India that connects investors with businesses seeking immediate cash flow. By funding invoices, investors earn returns while businesses meet their working capital needs. This chapter explores how invoice discounting works, its benefits, and how Indian investors can make the most of it.

1. Understanding Invoice Discounting

Invoice discounting is a short-term financing option where businesses sell their unpaid invoices at a discount to investors or financial institutions. Investors pay upfront and collect the full payment from customers later, earning returns through the discounted amount.

Key Features:

Short-term duration (30–90 days).

Low correlation with traditional market risks.

Direct support for small and medium enterprises (SMEs).

2. Why Invoice Discounting Appeals to Indian Investors

a. Stable Returns

Offers predictable returns due to fixed invoice amounts and timelines.

Ideal for conservative investors seeking consistent income.

b. Support for Local Businesses

Enables investors to contribute to the growth of India's SME sector.

Creates a win-win scenario for both parties.

c. Accessibility

Platforms like KredX and TradeCred have simplified entry points, allowing individuals to invest with as little as ₹50,000.

3. Risks and Rewards

Rewards:

High annualized returns (8–15% or more).

Low exposure to market volatility.

Risks:

Risk of customer default on invoice payments.

Limited regulation and investor protections in India.

Mitigation:

Choose credible platforms with rigorous credit-check mechanisms.

Diversify across multiple invoices to reduce default risk.

4. How to Get Started

Steps to Invest in Invoice Discounting:

Research platforms and choose one with a strong track record.

Register and complete the KYC process.

Browse available invoices and select based on credit ratings.

Invest in multiple invoices to diversify risks.

Monitor payments and reinvest returns.

5. The Future of Invoice Discounting in India

With the rise of fintech and digital lending platforms, invoice discounting is gaining traction in India. As regulation improves, it will become a mainstream alternative investment option for middle-class Indians seeking stable returns.

CHAPTER FOURTEEN

PEER-TO-PEER LENDING PLATFORMS: DEMOCRATIZING

Peer-to-peer (P2P) lending platforms connect borrowers with individual lenders, bypassing traditional financial institutions. This innovative model offers borrowers easy access to funds while providing lenders with higher returns compared to conventional savings instruments.

1. What is P2P Lending?

P2P lending involves individuals lending directly to other individuals or small businesses through online platforms. Lenders earn interest, while borrowers gain access to unsecured loans without the bureaucracy of banks.

Popular P2P Lending Platforms in India:

- Faircent
- LenDenClub

- RupeeCircle

2. Why P2P Lending is Gaining Popularity in India

a. High Returns

Lenders earn interest rates ranging from 10–30%, significantly higher than fixed deposits.

b. Customization

Lenders can choose borrowers based on risk profiles and credit scores.

c. Low Entry Barriers

Investments start as low as ₹5000, making it accessible to middle-class investors.

d. Digital Convenience

Entire process, from registration to payouts, is handled online.

3. Risks and Challenges in P2P Lending

a. Default Risk

Borrowers may fail to repay loans, leading to potential losses.

b. Regulatory Concerns

While RBI regulates P2P lending, it is still an evolving space in India.

c. Illiquidity

Investments are typically locked until loan repayment, reducing liquidity.

Mitigation:

Diversify investments across multiple borrowers.

Opt for platforms with robust credit-check mechanisms.

4. How to Start P2P Lending in India

Choose a Platform: Research and register with a trusted platform regulated by RBI.

Set Investment Goals: Decide on the amount and risk tolerance.

Review Borrower Profiles: Assess credit ratings, loan purposes, and repayment terms.

Invest Strategically: Spread your funds across multiple borrowers to minimize risks.

Monitor Returns: Track interest payments and reinvest earnings.

5. The Future of P2P Lending in India

As fintech adoption grows and trust in digital platforms increases, P2P lending will become a preferred investment avenue. For middle-class Indians, it offers a blend of accessibility, customization, and high returns, making it an attractive alternative to traditional savings options.

CHAPTER FIFTEEN

THE GOLDEN RULE – UNDERSTANDING RISKS BEFORE YOU INVEST

As we end this journey exploring alternative investments, it is crucial to step back and reflect on one fundamental truth: all investments carry risk. Whether stocks, real estate, private equity, or even alternative assets like cryptocurrencies and collectibles, every financial decision comes with uncertainties.

For many Indian investors, the traditional approach has always been safety first—fixed deposits, gold, and government bonds. While these instruments offer stability, they often lack the potential for higher returns. Alternatively, alternative investments open new doors for wealth creation but require a deeper understanding of risk, liquidity, and market fluctuations.

The Three Pillars of Smart Investing

Risk Awareness – Every investment has a risk-reward ratio. Higher returns often come with higher risks. Understand the risks before investing.

Due Diligence – Research, read, and verify. Whether it's a startup in private equity, a peer-to-peer lending platform, or an invoice discounting opportunity, always read the documents carefully.

Diversification – Never put all your money in one asset class. A balanced portfolio spreads risk and increases long-term stability.

Market Risks: The Unpredictable Factor

Economic downturns, inflation, interest rate changes, and even government regulations can impact investments. The alternative investment landscape in India is still evolving, and new policies or technological shifts may bring unexpected changes.

For instance:

- Cryptocurrencies are volatile and highly speculative.
- Real estate values fluctuate based on market cycles.
- Peer-to-peer lending carries the risk of defaults.
- Private equity and venture capital investments require patience and may take years to yield returns.

Understanding these risks helps you make informed decisions rather than being swayed by short-term market trends.

Final Words: Invest Wisely, Stay Informed

Investing is not just about multiplying wealth—it's about making smart, informed choices that align with your goals and risk tolerance. Whether you are a beginner or an experienced investor, the key to success is education, patience, and adaptability.

Before making any investment, always read all offer documents carefully, analyze the risks, and consult a financial expert if necessary. Remember, financial growth is a journey, not a sprint.

By combining traditional wisdom with modern opportunities, you can create a future-proof financial strategy and take control of your wealth.

Ctrl+Alt=Wealth is now in your hands. Make the right moves, and let your wealth journey begin!

Happy investing!
-Sidda Raviteja